The Pocket Book of God

Ehssan Sakhaee, PhD

Contents

Preface

This book is a short guide to returning to our true Source, God. It is a reminder of our depth of need in the Essence of our very existence and to remember and return to our Source, each time we forget and become aware of this forgetfulness, which is generally characterized by some level of inner suffering such as anxiety, stress, loneliness, disconnection to name a few. It is hoped that it provides a pointer to the practice of constantly returning to God's Presence, every time one suffers through forgetfulness of God. To remember, trust and surrender in God, at all times.

It is hoped that you uncover the uncaused deep sense of inner peace by practicing the content of this book. I'd like to emphasise that the practice of *remembrance* is essential, and this book acts as a guide and pointer for this actual practice.

God the Source

God is all that there is. God is the Source, from which all else emanates. All that exists emanates from God. God is the Source of All things and beyond. God is beyond imagination. God's presence pervades everything.

Everything emanates from God and God pervades all things. God is the Infinite. The Ultimate Truth that cannot be conceived by the mind or beliefs. Every belief system points to God and yet the description, the pointer is tainted by the limitation of the limited vocabulary and human conception. For how can one understand the Infinite, that is God?

All things are from Thee, for Thee and because of Thee. There is only one perpetual existence and the cause of all existence that surpasses all else.

As God is the Source, all is from Thee. Whatever wonder has manifested and manifests in this world that is worth of praise, is attributed to God. This includes natural wonders as well as human accomplishments. One can never again be proud of anything great one does as all that is great and beneficent is manifested from God. Every time you or someone does wondrous and magnificent things, you praise God for this magnificence is a manifestation from God, and so praise be to God.

All creation is the medium that manifests Infinite qualities. Everything comes from the Source.

God permeates the causal world - though God is in the realm of non-causation. There is no cause for God, though God is the cause of all causal phenomenon and non-causal phenomenon. God is all that there is. And the causal realm is an illusion and temporary, changing.

Prayer: God, You are all that there is. You are the Alpha and the Omega and beyond.

God's Love

The only stable constant perpetual, pervasive infinite love that there is, was and that will ever be is God's Infinite and Omnipresent Love. People you may love will come and go, animals, including your dog, comes and goes, everything is impermanent, ephemeral and everchanging except God's omnipresent and infinite love.

How does one breathe without God's constant loving presence? The answer is simple. One doesn't. God's Love spans all things. God's Love is the basis of everything else. It is where one returns to for healing and rejuvenation. God's love is vast and permeates all time and space. When one removes any obstacles to this Love, one can experience this perpetual everlasting omnipresent love. You can then become the mirror of this Love and shine it upon all that you come across, you shine the Light of God upon the Earth and all its inhabitants.

How can you receive God's love if you are not allowing God's love to be channelled through you?

God's love is always there, but to experience it, you must allow it to flow outwards towards the world. The more you channel God's love towards the world and yourself the more you feel the presence of God's love. It is always there, only masked by the mind. Without the mind,

God's Infinite Love can be experienced. Stillness and total presence is required to access this. Awareness of the body, breath and the heart are direct channels to this.

Prayer: God, fill us with your Infinite Love, for Your Love is the Source of All Love and we infinitely in deep need of Your Love.

God's Omnipresence

God's constant loving presence permeates all of existence. When you recognize and realise that God's Presence is in every atom, in every cell, in every speck of your own being and everything that there is, then how can you ever be disconnected from God? You are totally submerged in God's Presence, completely and at all times, in the Eternal. God's Presence exceeds all existence, it permeates all time and space, it is permanent, perpetual into eternity. Everything contains God's Essence and Presence. From the tiny ant, the bird, the tree, and every single human being on this planet, contains the Essence, often veiled by form, by ego and by judgement. When judgement subsides, you see God's Face in everything.

Essentially there is nothing else, but God and God alone there is. All else is veil.

Prayer: God, You are all that there is. All else is veil. Help us see through the veil of this world of forms, and help us remember that You are all that there is. In everything, there is Your Essence. Your Presence.

God's Omniscient

God's Omnipresence leads to God's Omniscience. Absolute Knowledge. God is the Knower of All Things and beyond. Recognising this Truth, sets you free from thinking that you know what is best for you or others. This leads to *surrendering* to the All Knowing. This realisation gives you access to *trust.* Since God is All Knowing and in the best position to make judgements, you trust God's judgement beyond your own or any other. Our limited perspective, knowledge and understanding will continue to limit us from clear and objective justifiable judgment. Thus

---

Prayer: God, You are the Knower of All Things and in the best place to judge, knowing what is best for, us, and the world. Let us relinquish our judgement, and trust in You and You alone. Guide us Lord so that we do what is aligned with Truth and in line with the True Knowledge that you have. Impart wisdom and knowledge to us so that we may know better and make better decisions aligned with Your Will.

God as the Owner

God owns all. Everything we have is temporarily in our presence and we are responsible for what is in our temporal possession.

You and I and everything that there was, is, and will be, are completely owned by God. There exist no no partial ownership. It is a complete and total ownership. For God owns everything, and so you and I are completely God's and God's alone we are. God owns our bodies, minds, hearts, souls, our relationships, our possessions. Everything known and unknown is from God, and for God – completely owned by God. All that ever existed, exists, and will ever exist, all that can be seen and unseen, belongs to God.

Since we and everything that there completely belong to God, there is no other true belonging other than the one belonging (to God). This is the ultimate and complete belonging. One's complete being and all that ever is, belongs to Thee.

Since God owns everything, there is nothing to be owned, all is owned by God, and God alone. Thus, clinging onto anything, which is always arising and passing, comes and going in form, is ultimately futile. Possessions, relationships, your own ephemeral body, all arise and pass away. You will then welcome the arising and passing, the coming and going, the beginning and ending of all things including your own life and everything you may have in your possession. You also recognise your responsibly to take care of what has been gifted or granted to you for whatever duration it is gifted or granted to you. You are effectively custodians of what

---

Prayer: God, I am completely owned by You, and You alone. All that I am and all that I have is Yours, and Yours alone. God, all that there is, is Yours and Yours alone. We own nothing, yet we are custodians of everything. Help and guide us so that we take care of what have the capacity to take care of in the time that we are custodians of what is all Yours.

God's Will

When you realise that God is the owner of all things and the knower of all things, you will naturally surrender to God's will. Since an individual nor a collective could ever know enough about all things, and so nobody will ever be in a position to know what is best, the surrender to God's Will is inevitable. You will know that all will be God's Will.

God's Will always overrides all other wills. God's Will comes first and all else later.

Submitting to the Will of God helps you relinquish control and surrender fully. You experience true freedom here.

Whenever you feel any signs of negativity such as disappointment, regret, or anxiety, it is sign that you are not in full surrender. You have forgotten to fully trust and let go. Through a declaration or prayer you can restore yourself to the state of full surrender.

Prayer: God, Your Will shall always surpass mine and all. Your Will and Your Will alone, reigns supreme. We surrender to Your Will.

God's Guidance

Since God is the Knower of all things and God's Will reigns supreme, one naturally asks God for guidance, so that one's attention, mind, body, heart and soul are aligned with God's Will and directed in the path best known by God, for the good of all. One surrenders to God's Will and asks for guidance to think and act in the right direction. Control is relinquished and surrendering to God's Guidance and Will takes over. You will then look for signs, and allow the soul to align and direct your life and your actions. Your ego's temporary desires begin to subsite naturally and without effort.

Prayer: Lord, guide me for I need Your guidance at all times. Guide my heart, mind, and body in the right path, so that I do what is right, what is good and what is aligned with Your Will.

God's Manifestation

Reflect on God's manifested qualities in everyday life. Become God's mirror so that you shine through those qualities in this world. If you have role models this can help. If you ask yourself: what are God's qualities and what are the qualities of the Prophets. How do you cultivate and manifest these qualities within yourself and become the representatives of these qualities?

Qualities of Mercy, Compassion, Benevolence, how do you allow these qualities to come into the world through you, by becoming more merciful, compassionate and benevolent?

Prayer: Lord, use me to shine your infinite qualities through my thoughts, words and actions, and my being. Fill me with Your qualities so that I can shine unto the world the Infinite Light that You are. And may all praise be to You for anything I manifest, for I am only your tool, and nothing of my own.

God's Servant

As you become totally immersed in God, you naturally take on the role of God's Servant. You become nothing but God's and only exist for God's purpose and service. You may not know exactly how the Lord will use you but you will in time know and begin to act in the service of the Lord. You will be guided towards what needs to be done for God's sake. You will lose all need for your own personal life, your selfish needs diminish and you will truly feel like nothing but the servant of God. You will begin to enter the realm of nothingness, true humility, and experience God's total Presence and guidance within you. As your role of total nothingness begins to unfold you enter the realm of Everything. Everything becomes part of you and you become part of Everything and at the service of all that there is. There is no separation once you arrive here, which is accessible, *now* and *here*. You are in fact *now* annihilated in God. At the dept of your being, nothing else exists, but God. This is no longer a thought or a belief. It is Reality.

Prayer: Lord, use me as you will in whatever way you wish to use me. For I am Yours and Yours alone and I serve You, and serve You alone.

The Divine Connection

Since you are now connected to the Infinite Source, your need in the *world of forms* diminishes, but it is only now that you can give without needing, it is only now you can give selflessly and with a sense of total freedom. You realise your giving is not from you, but God uses you to give to what is the God's, that also includes you in that ownership.

We appreciate and feel grateful for the love and attention from others, and all the wonderful things that we may have in our possessions and all of our experiences. However, there is no longer a need or clinging to anything of this world. All comes and goes away, arises and passes away. Since all *things* will in time, come and go, and what remains is your deep connection with the Source, your Essence. Here, you are grounded in God. You may still have desires, but your desires are softer and gentler, and often at the periphery of your life rather than the centre. This is because your primary purpose is service and your primary source of joy and peace, is God. We may desire connection with others but in the absence of this, we don't break and fall apart as we are connected to infinite source of love and care. You receive God's love anywhere and everywhere, and no matter who you are and what circumstances you have, taking refuge in God's presence and love reminds you of your deep inherent connection with the Source, the Divine

Presence that permeates all things, and the only true eternal connection.

When we do recognise God's pervasive perpetual presence, all fear including fear of loneliness, rejection, loss and abandonment diminishes. We become more secure in stepping into God's perpetual and pervasive Presence and Infinite Love.

Prayer: Lord, help us remember our deep connection with You, our Source and that all other connections are temporal, while the connection with You, eternal.

The Need for God

On realisation of how God is essentially all, the Source and the Light of our existence, one recognises the perpetual deep need in God at every split moment in time. To the point that this need exceeds every other need (that is form), even more than what is needed for immediate physical survival (e.g. air). The one When one's need in God exceeds that of the basic needs for physical survival, and that of life itself then one is completely submerged and annihilated in the presence of God. There is nothing else.

All human needs can be measured. The amount of oxygen you need to survive, the amount of nutrition to function and live. All physical needs are measurable.

The infinite dimension of God reflects *infinite need.*

An infinite need in God is a need beyond measure. It cannot be comprehended as the degree of this need is beyond measure. Since the *Container* and what *Beholds* all existence is the *Infinite Sustainer* of what is, what has been, and what can be.

Needing God in three dimensions of the past (forgiveness), present (love), and future (guidance). The need for God is beyond the mind, beyond belief and beyond comprehension. This need is endless, perpetual, and infinitely deep. It is so deep that words cannot describe. The need for God is beyond the need for air, as you may need air every few seconds, you need God every split of a moment. Needing God does not make a person good or bad. It simply reflects a person's deep need of God, period. Anyone can be in deep need of God, anyone indeed. You do not need to believe in anything or be anything to be a deep needer of God (DNOG).

In life you inevitably experience various degrees of pain from mild uneasiness to intense deep emotional pain. This of course could be from loss, from shock, or trauma. Being in pain is natural and the suffering is real. There is no blame. It is simply asking us to recognise that your need in God is real, so declare your deep need in God in this moment of pain. The more intense the pain, the more intense your need. Soften your body and imagine your body as a translucent vessel needing to be filled with God's Love. Turn to your Lord and humbly ask to be filled with the God's Love.

You can begin to recognise the depth of your need in God, a depth of need that is beyond measure, beyond belief. It is as though you need God more than you need to breathe. The intensity of this depth of need cannot be put into words. As the depth of your need in God has increased, the depth of need for other things (other than God) decreases. You begin to experience freedom from the world, from mind and matter.

To realise and recognise the depth of need and simultaneously the depth of presence, permeating all time and space, you begin to dissolve into this depth and the intense joy and love arising from the Infinite, arising from this total submergence fills you up *completely*. Wherever you turn, it is *there*.

You realise that every breath you take is *from* The Source and *returning* to the Source. You realise you need the Source for every breath and this depth of need becomes clear and apparent at every level of your being. You are now consumed and completely annihilated, in God.

This intoxication in God, arises as the experience of the infinite presence of love that has no object to project towards. The feeling is just there without any images circulating the mind, giving rise to an uncaused joy, love and peace within.

Prayer: God, I need You and I need You more than life. I need Your forgiveness of the past, Your Love in the present, and Your guidance in the future.

Remembrance and Returning to God

When you forget your deep need in God, the Infinite, you will begin to resort to needing worldly things, material things, relationships, circumstances to give you a temporarily feeling of security and worth. You have forgotten the only Source that quenches all your needs that is available to you, always.

Any sign of disturbed inner peace is a sign of the ego arising, masking the presence of the Lord within you. Become present. Observe the ego arising with vigilance, with total alertness, with curiosity and with love. The ego will not prevail or gain strength in your deep alert presence. You will return to the Divine's presence within you.

All evil all ego are of the same quality of various degrees and the consequences may also vary but essentially, it's the same: forgetfulness of God that leads to sinking into unconsciousness, being carried away by the ego.

The mere leaving God's Presence is the beginning of suffering.

Every time we experience pain and suffering, we are in the presence of *forgetfulness* or *unawareness* - we have already forgotten God. We have forgotten to put ourselves totally in the Presence of God, to trust and surrender in God, in God's Will, and God's Way.

There is a process of returning to God, when you fall into unconsciousness and become forgetful of God.

We have the **AAAAH** process as follows:

1. Awareness of unconsciousness
2. Acknowledge and admit it
3. 3.Ask for forgiveness from God (repentance and redemption)
4. Arrive in God's Presence
5. Heal through God's Infinite Love Become aware of the ego obstructing God's infinite Love and Grace. Acknowledge and admit your unconsciousness, your ego that has taken over, immediately asking for God's forgiveness and love. You may arrive in God's presence, with God's grace. Find any obstacle that there may be to God's Infinite Love. God is always ready to forgive, but you may be obstructing it through guilt and shame. Notice this and remove this veil to God's infinite Love.

When we genuinely and authentically remember God, with the *intention* of simply remembering, rather than the intention of feeling good or being relieved of suffering, we experience God's Peace. The three stages of *Remembrance*

1. *Remember* God (through prayer, contemplation, awareness)
2. *Return* to God's Presence (feel God's Presence within you, in every cell of your body, heart, and mind and in every aspect of life, and all of Existence)
3. *Remain* in God's Presence (continue this awareness for as long as possible)

When you remember God, become deeply grateful for this remembrance. Remaining in God's Presence may pose the biggest challenge. This is because the ego always lurks in our lives and very close to us and can take us away from God's Presence. Total alert awareness and consciousness is necessary to remain in God's Love and God's Light. Every source of suffering is a sign of forgetfulness and a call to return and remember.

Prayer: God, every cell and every atom of my body and every speck of my being is filled with You – with your Light and with Your Love. Help us remember You, always for every forgetfulness of Your Presence, leads to suffering. Help us remember, return and remain in Your Presence, Lord, always.

Immersion and Annihilation in God

To become totally immersed in God, to become completely God's and nothing else but the Lord's. It is euphoria and the more of *nothingness* you become the more you can experience it. If you seek this for the sake of the feeling, then come not this way, as it is only for the true lovers that want to burn and dissolve in God. If you come just for God and you are prepared to become *nothing* without any expectations, then come through. You will know how pure your intention is. When you recognise that there is essentially nothing else but God, that all other things are simply details, of the ephemeral reality of the rising and the passing of forms, , you will remember that you are completely grounded in God. Everything else is details, a divine dance you play while you are here, until you return to your King, finally. Your origin. Your true home.

When God's living presence permeates every aspect, every cell, every atom, every moment of your being. There is total submergence, total presence, total annihilation in God. When there is nothing else, but God. All else is veil. Wherever you turn, there is nothing, but God. Completely consumed in Thee. Total belonging, total surrender. Nothing even gets remotely close to this experience. The experience of totally being consumed in God. No love story, no romance, no magnificent vacation can ever come close to *this* experience, the experience of totally being consumed in the Divine Light that essentially permeates everything that there is, the total intoxication in God. Many have not yet even glimpsed this reality, and some have done so only very briefly, only to return to the ephemeral - their dominant state. When you experience the Omnipresent Love that permeates everything, you first realise how deeply you are in need of this and also simultaneously realising how it is everywhere, and accessible at anytime by you and everyone, and everything that there is. It has always been there and always will be - beyond physical forms, beyond survival, beyond your mortal and ephemeral body and mind and beyond all of *existence*, for all existence is inherently, ephemeral, arising and passing.

Prayer: Let us be consumed in Your Presence, let us become fully submerged in You – intoxicated in You - for You are all that there is and nothing else there is.

About the Author

Ehssan had a prophetic dream at the age 12 of a message to be delivered from the Most High. He tried to ignore this having a deep interest in the sciences and pursued an engineering and academic career. Though he kept being drawn to spirituality at various times in his life, from mid to late teens and then again in his late 20s, which began to unfold new layers within him. Over the next decade in his 30s the signs and messages became stronger until he had no choice to write about them, despite his lack of formal education in theology and his questioning of who he was to do this. He considers himself as *nothing* but the servant of the One God, the Eternal.

www.ingramcontent.com/pod-product-compliance
Lightning Source LLC
La Vergne TN
LVHW041307150826
845673LV00008B/2773

* 9 7 9 8 3 6 3 6 2 4 4 6 9 *